TO NEW BABY BEN

2014

The Kuekumber Kids™ meet THE MONSTER OF MANNERS

Written and Illustrated by

Scott E. Sutton

There's a party at the Kuekumber's. Why, you say?

'Cause today is Katy Kuekumber's birthday.

But Katy is mad, and as you might guess,

Her birthday party has become a big mess.

There are kids throwing cake all over the place.
A piece just hit Katy right in the face.
There is ice cream and candy all over the floor,
And Katy's poor mom can't take any more.

Katy Kuekumber was about to yell

When she heard "ding, dong" from the front door bell.

Her mom opened the door and to their surprise

Stood a very strange monster of a very large size.

He had skin that was blue and hair that was yellow,

And he wasn't messy, but a nicely dressed fellow.

He wore a neat suit with a bow tie, too.

He even smelled good, not like an old shoe.

"YIKES!" yelled Katy. "First kids throw my cake.

Now a MONSTER shows up. Oh, what a mistake!"

"Do not fear," said the monster, "I will not hurt you.

Your party's a mess, but I know what to do."

"Allow me," he said, "to tell you my name.

I'm the Monster of Manners and it is my aim

To save your party. I know why it's a mess.

Because no one has learned their MANNERS, I'd guess."

"Manners? Manners? What are manners?" asked Lance,
Who was wiping some cake off his colorful pants.
"Manners," said Monster, "show you how to treat others,
Like friends and parents, your sisters and brothers."

"Now to help me teach these manners to you
Are the Manners Monsters, Bubby and Shmoo."
"Greetings to you!" the monsters did holler.
They were monsters all right, but quite a bit smaller.

"Fix my party?" asked Katy. "Okay, go ahead."

"No problem. Call me Manny," the big monster said.

"Now the first bunch of manners is how to be clean,

'Cause this is the worst mess I've ever seen!"

"Okay, kids," said Manny, "we'll start with the floor.
We'll clean this place up 'til the mess is no more."
So they cleaned up the cake and the candy, too,
And the ice cream and presents until they were through.

When cleaning the mess up was finally done,
He said, "Wash your hands and face everyone."
"But why wash up?" asked Kirky. "How come?
We're gonna get dirty again, that's dumb!"

"Some people," said Manny, "may say 'Don't be picky.

You can smell bad, stay dirty and gooey and icky.'

But there is a secret you really must know.

When things stay dirty GERMS can grow."

"Germs? What are germs?" Katy asked quickly.

"They're tiny little bugs that can make you quite sickly.

They're so small you can't see them," Manny did say.

"Where there's dirt and bad smells they're not far away."

"Wash your hands and face after you play.

Take a bath or a shower every day.

Cover your mouth when you cough or you sneeze

Or you'll spray germs on people, so don't do that, please!"

"When you sneeze or have stuff stuck in your nose,

Use a tissue to clean it, not your fingers or clothes.

Flush the toilet, too. Wash your hands when you're through.

'Cause there are germs in the toilet and it stinks! P.U.!"

"YIKES!" said Kirky. "That's why you keep clean,
Because of those germs that can't be seen."
"Right," said the monster, "but wait, there's more!
When you leave things a mess on the table or floor,"

"Like clothes or food, your toys and all,
People can trip on them, slip and fall.
If your room is a mess," Manny told everyone,
"You can't find a thing or get anything done!"

"You look for some crayons. Oh, where could they be?

But to find them at all takes a day, maybe three!

It's okay to work and play and have fun,

But clean up and pick up your stuff when you're done."

"Now line up for cake, kids," Manny did say.

"I'll teach you to get things done the right way."

Kids were pushing and yelling for cake and ice cream.

"PLEASE BE QUIET!" Monster Bubby did scream.

The kids became quiet with a look of surprise.

Bubby's voice was so loud for the monster's small size!

"If you all interrupt when someone is talking,

You can't hear a thing. It's like chickens are squawking!"

"Here are some manners you've got to learn.

Don't all go at once. You must each wait your turn.

If you all go at once you will smoosh everyone.

Then no one gets nothin' and nothin' gets done!"

"Say PLEASE if you want something done, it's true.
Like 'Please may I have cake and ice cream, too?'
And when someone gives or does something for you
Always say THANK YOU to them when they're through."

The kids and the monsters each got some cake,

Saying PLEASE and THANK YOU without a mistake.

"Close your mouth and don't talk whenever you chew,

Or the food will fall out and that's gross!" said Shmoo.

"What about burping?" asked Kirky Kuekumber.

"Your burps," laughed Katy, "are loud like thunder!"

"Cover your mouth when you burp," Bubby said.

"Don't make them so loud. Say EXCUSE ME instead."

"Here's a manner," said Manny, "that's helpful to know.
You can use EXCUSE ME wherever you go.
To get through a crowd or cross through a line,
Say EXCUSE ME first. You'll get through just fine."

"If you meet your friends or someone new,
Smile and say HELLO," said Shmoo.
"Then, when you leave, you always should say
GOOD-BYE to them before walking away."

When the kids and the monsters ate and were done
They went outside to play games and have fun.
They played soccer, jump rope and baseball, too.
But the monsters saw there was more work to do.

Some kids playing ball started yelling and fighting.

They were using bad words, even hitting and biting!

Some girls had taken one of Katy's new toys,

And poor Krumby's tail was being pulled by some boys.

Krumby was growling. Katy started to cry.
It was time to give some new manners a try.
So Manny the Monster, with Bubby and Shmoo,
Went out to show the kids what to do.

The Monster of Manners said, "Listen here, boys.
Don't hurt that poor dog. He's not one of your toys.
How would you like someone to do that to you?
Be nice to animals, they'll be nice to you, too."

"Now girls," he said, "taking things isn't fair.
If you ask Katy nicely, maybe she'll share."
"Don't take people's stuff without asking," said Shmoo.
"Ask first and say PLEASE. It's the right thing to do."

Manny the Monster told the boys playing ball,

"These bad words and hitting are no good at all!"

"Don't hit or hurt people," said Bubby and Shmoo,

"'Cause you wouldn't want them to hit or hurt you."

"If you hurt people's feelings, call them names that are bad,
You will lose them as friends and then you'll be sad.
If you really want people to be nice to you,
You've got to try to be nice to them, too."

"If someone gets hurt, like falls to the ground,
Don't laugh or make fun, don't just stand around.
Make sure they're all right and if they're not okay,
Then go get some help for them right away."

"All people are different, not just different clothes,

Their bodies different colors, a big or small nose.

Some may be skinny and some may be tubby,

But they're people like you are," said Monster Bubby.

"If you want others to be nice to you,

Try to use manners and be nice to them, too."

"Good-bye!" said Manny, Bubby and Shmoo.

"You've now learned your manners. You know what to do."

"Thanks for your help," happy Katy did say.

"You're welcome!" said the monsters who went on their way.

She went back to her party. It was much better now.

How come? They were using MANNERS, that's how.

The Kuekumber Kids ...

Katy

Kirky

Lance

Krumby

For more books by Scott E. Sutton visit *www.ScottESutton.com*

Do you have these books by Scott E. Sutton?

How to Draw Stuff™

The Family of Ree™ Adventures

The Family of Ree
The Secret of Gorbee Grotto
Look at the Size of That Long-Legged Ploot!
The Legend of Snow Pookas

The Adventures Dinosaur Dog™

Tyrannosaurus Forest
Danger: Dinky Diplodocus
Trouble with Pteranodons
Death by Deinonychus

www.ScottESutton.com

The Kuekumber Kids Meet™ The Monster of Manners
Second Edition © 2012 by Scott E. Sutton
First Edition © 1997 by Scott E. Sutton

ISBN: 978-0-9851061-0-2
Second Edition
Printed in the USA
Design and layout by Susie Sutton
Manufactured by Thomson-Shore, Dexter, MI (USA); RMA583TB509, July, 2012